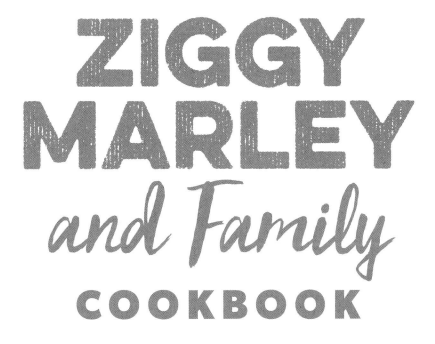

ZIGGY MARLEY
and Family
COOKBOOK

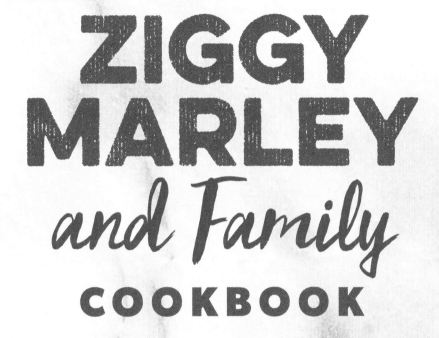

ZIGGY MARLEY
and Family
COOKBOOK

**DELICIOUS MEALS MADE WITH WHOLE,
ORGANIC INGREDIENTS
FROM THE MARLEY KITCHEN**

AKASHIC BOOKS   TUFF GONG WORLDWIDE

Tuff Gong Worldwide and the Tuff Gong Worldwide logo are
trademarks of the Robert Marley Foundation, under exclusive
license by Tuff Gong Worldwide LLC.

Published by Akashic Books
©2016 Tuff Gong Worldwide

ISBN: 978-1-671775-483-8
Library of Congress Control Number: 2016935088

Printed in China

Akashic Books
Twitter: @AkashicBooks
Facebook: AkashicBooks
E-mail: info@akashicbooks.com
Website: www.akashicbooks.com

Tuff Gong Worldwide
Twitter: @tuffgongww
Facebook/Instagram: Tuff Gong Worldwide
Websites: www.tuffgongworldwide.com, www.ziggymarley.com

To my family, Mother Earth,
and all of you . . .
Cook and live life with purpose.

CONTENTS

ABOUT ORGANIC INGREDIENTS

I am an advocate of sustainable, organic foods and transparent labeling on food packaging. It's what inspired us to start Ziggy Marley Organics. While I stress GMO-free ingredients, I understand that these foods may not be available to everyone, by location or cost. The important thing is to be aware of what you're putting in your body and support local, organic growers whenever you may be able. Many of the recipes in this cookbook are vegetarian, vegan, and/or gluten-free, so we have indicated this near the top of each respective page.

FOOD PAIRINGS AND RECOMMENDATIONS

I like to mix and match nearly everything in here. For example, I love eating the tuna burger without the bun. Instead, I top it with the Caribbean Salsa, Quinoa Salad, and some leftover sauce and spices from the Curry Escovitch. Have fun with it, be creative, and find me online—let me know what type of pairings you create.

Ziggy

I first started dabbling in the kitchen as a teenager. I enjoyed making cornmeal porridge, and it helped me to begin appreciating the idea of nourishment, the idea that food can make your body feel better. I would make Irish moss and some of my dad's juices. I grew up around great cooks, especially my mother, my great-auntie Viola, and Ms. Collins, a woman who helped us out around the house. But no one taught me how to cook—I just watched and made things up as I went.

Matter of fact, the first food I ever remember eating was fruit from a tree. In some ways, fruit picked from a tree is the most basic kind of meal there is. Where I grew up there were mango trees, cherry trees, many different fruit trees. This was in Bull Bay, an area of Jamaica to the southeast of Kingston, where my family moved in 1972.

Bull Bay had a very rural kind of vibe, a community vibe. Most of the food came from the garden. We had some chickens—eating chicken was special back then, not an everyday thing. We also had a goat, and when my father's music got more popular we expanded to three or four goats. The nicest meals you ever got was on Sundays. Sundays you were going to get dumplings in the morning, maybe rice and peas later in the day.

Our Rasta culture was different than regular Jamaican culture. We used to have both sides then, because my auntie would cook the more traditional Jamaican food. On the other side, our Rasta culture drew us to a different way of eating. My father would always have a lot of juices and greens and nuts. We were introduced to ital food—fresh, organic, and nutritious, less salt. We were basically eating kosher food in those days. We ate chicken and red meat.

Fortunately, healthy food can be found almost everywhere now. Back when I was a younger musician, I used to try some of that truck stop food when I was on tour, but not anymore. These days, my livet (diet) doesn't really change when I go on the road.

The food of my youth, and my wife Orly's, continues to be the food of our adulthood. An Israeli of Iranian descent, Orly really understands food and family. She grew up with a stable family structure, and she places a high value on family meals. We eat a lot of Persian and Israeli food at home. We celebrate Shabbat every week, along with Jewish holidays like Passover and Hanukkah. All of this has taught me even more about the relationship between food and family.

My own upbringing was much more loose when it came to meals. Some evenings my auntie would be in the house working while my mom and dad were on the road, so we'd just be playing marbles or other games when mealtime came. My parents made sure we never went hungry, but sometimes me and my friends found ourselves roaming around Bull Bay with empty bellies, foraging and eating off trees. I remember a few times when we would shoot down a bird with a slingshot and then just cook it right up. You won't find that recipe here.

In 2013 we started a company called Ziggy Marley Organics, offering a line of hempseeds and the world's first flavored coconut oils, which are important ingredients in the food we eat. It was the very positive response to Ziggy Marley Organics that first planted the seed in my mind to harvest a family cookbook, inspired by the food of my life.

Many of the recipes in this book are my versions of the ital food and Jamaican meals that we ate growing up and still do today. Other recipes have been contributed by my wife Orly, my daughter Judah, my sister Karen, Chef Bruce Sherman, Chef Ben Ford, Chef Leonie McDonald, Chef Ricardo A. Rodríguez, Lea Kabani, my mother-in-law Polin Agai, and Matt Solodky. All the recipes have a special emphasis on nourishment and love, because nothing works without love . . . even food.

The cookbook is organized around different times of the day, though I have tried to break out of the traditional breakfast/lunch/dinner mind-set. Instead, the recipes are grouped into sections called Rise, All Day, Midday, Evening, and Sweets.

We hope you enjoy these recipes as much as we do. And if we've succeeded in what we're trying to do here, your body will thank your taste buds. Always listen to your body, always trust your body. It speaks to you. Food and family.

I'm a breakfast person. It's the most important meal for me, and eggs were the first food I learned to cook. If I wanted to make an omelet, that was easy. If I wanted to make an omelet with something different to it, that was easy too. When I was growing up, they used to feed me a lot of eggs. There was this lady who brought my auntie eggs from her chickens every morning. I suppose it was for me specially she would bring them. Every other day there'd be boiled eggs or fried eggs or scrambled. This is why the first recipe in the book is my Egg Sandwich with Avocado Spread (page 15).

I also like pancakes, and so does my family, but they don't have any real nourishment other than the eggs. One day I said to my son, "You know what, today we're not making pancakes. We're making Mancakes" (page 16). Mancakes got more to it than just flour and water. Mancakes got to nourish. We put coconut oil in them, some pumpkin seeds, flaxseeds, chia seeds, sometimes walnuts. On Saturday mornings I'll make my kids Mancakes with maple syrup as a treat.

Oatmeal—that's my go-to meal right there. It has protein and everything else in it you need. My wife Orly's oatmeal (page 21) guarantees you will start your day feeling nice and strong. And that's the point: the recipes in this section will nourish you to start the day smiling. Smiling with the rising sun.

"Eggs were the first food I learned to cook. When I was growing up, they used to feed me a lot of eggs. There was this lady who brought my auntie eggs from her chickens every morning."

EGG SANDWICH WITH AVOCADO SPREAD

Sandwich serves 1, with extra spread,
Vegetarian

PREPARATION

Fry plantains in 1 tablespoon coconut oil and 4 tablespoons olive oil. Fry at medium heat until plantains start to become golden brown.

Fry eggs in 1/2 tablespoon butter and 1 tablespoon olive oil.

Toast bread, apply avocado spread, and layer with lettuce, tomatoes, fried plantains, and eggs.

Add salt and pepper to taste.

AVOCADO SPREAD PREPARATION

Mix and mash all the ingredients together and spread away.

INGREDIENTS

1 plantain, peeled and sliced into
   1/2-inch pieces
1 tablespoon Ziggy Marley's
   Coco'Mon Coconut Oil, or
   coconut oil of your choosing
2 eggs
1/2 tablespoon butter
5 tablespoons olive oil
2 slices sourdough bread, or your
   favorite bread
2 butter lettuce leaves
2 slices heirloom tomato
Salt and cracked pepper, to taste

AVOCADO SPREAD
2 avocados
Salt and pepper, to taste
1 teaspoon fresh lemon juice, or to
   taste

MANCAKES

Serves 3 to 4, Vegetarian/Gluten-Free

INGREDIENTS

2 cups flour, or substitute
  gluten-free flour
2 tablespoons brown sugar
1/2 teaspoon salt
3 teaspoons baking powder
1 tablespoon pumpkin seeds,
  crushed
1 tablespoon flaxseeds
1 tablespoon chia seeds
1 tablespoon walnuts, crushed
2 eggs, beaten
4 tablespoons Ziggy Marley's
  Coco'Mon Coconut Oil, or
  coconut oil of your choosing
2 cups water, or substitute coconut,
  soy, almond, rice, or whole milk

PREPARATION

Mix all dry ingredients together, then add eggs, coconut oil, and water and blend well.

Spoon batter onto a hot grill.

Once pancakes bubble, flip over and cook until golden brown.

Serve with maple syrup and enjoy!

Mancakes got more to it than just flour
and water. Mancakes got to nourish.
On Saturday mornings I'll make my kids
Mancakes with maple syrup as a treat."

GIDEON'S FAVORITE BANANA MUFFINS

Yields 6 to 8 muffins, Vegetarian

INGREDIENTS

1 large banana (or 2 small), very ripe, mashed
1 egg plus enough milk to make 1 cup liquid combined (coconut, rice, almond, or soy milk optional)
1/2 cup Ziggy Marley's Coco'Mon Coconut Oil, or coconut oil of your choosing
1 teaspoon vanilla
1 1/2 cups flour (gluten-free flour optional)
1 cup sugar
1 teaspoon baking soda
Optional: nuts, banana slices, and chocolate chips

PREPARATION

Preheat oven to 350°F.

Combine all ingredients in a large bowl.

Use electric mixer on slow to medium until lumps are pretty well gone.

Slather muffin pan with more coconut oil.

Bake for approximately 10–15 minutes for smaller muffins, and 15–25 minutes for larger muffins; do a toothpick test for doneness.

Enjoy!

BREAKFAST HASH
WITH ASPARAGUS SAUCE

Serves 4 to 6, Vegetarian/Vegan/Gluten-Free

INGREDIENTS

4 large sweet potatoes, diced
2 tablespoons olive oil
1 yellow onion, diced
4 large beets, diced
Optional: smoked salmon, chicken sausage, or other protein of your choosing
Salt and pepper, to taste
Rosemary sprig

SAUCE
1/2 pound asparagus
3 cloves garlic, crushed
2 cups milk, nondairy preferred (rice milk or almond milk)
4 tablespoons olive oil
2 tablespoons agave sweetener
Salt and pepper, to taste
1 bunch mint

PREPARATION

Preheat oven to 425°F.

Roast sweet potatoes in oven for 30 minutes.

While potatoes are cooking, heat olive oil at medium-high in a large frying pan. Add onions to pan, sautéing until near brown (about 15 minutes).

Add diced beets and cook on medium heat while potatoes finish in oven.

Add roasted sweet potatoes and diced cooked protein (if desired) to frying pan. Mix, season with salt and pepper, to taste.

Reduce heat to low, drizzle with olive oil, and lay sprig of rosemary on top. Cover and keep warm for 10 minutes.

In a large pot, braise asparagus and garlic: Add a tablespoon of olive oil to pot and warm over medium-high heat. Add asparagus and garlic, and cook until the asparagus flesh begins in blister in spots. Add nondairy milk, agave, salt, and pepper. Bring to a boil, then simmer until the asparagus and garlic soften, about 10 –12 minutes, depending on the thickness of the asparagus. Add more milk as needed to reach desired consistency (a smooth, creamy, silklike texture).

Add mint and cook off excess liquid. There should be slightly more asparagus than milk.

Blend into a smooth sauce. Add more nondairy milk for desired sauce consistency.

Remove rosemary from hash, serve in bowls, and top with sauce.

"Oatmeal—that's my go-to meal right there. It has protein and everything else in it you need. My wife Orly's oatmeal guarantees you will start your day feeling nice and strong."

OATMEAL

Serves 1, Vegetarian/Vegan/Gluten-Free

PREPARATION

Prepare oats with wet ingredients or according to package directions.

Top with blueberries, walnuts (or pumpkin seeds), flaxseeds, coconut, banana, and optional golden berries—and enjoy!

INGREDIENTS

1 cup oats, either quick cooking or old-fashioned rolled (can be pre-soaked overnight)

2 cups water, or substitute coconut, soy, almond, rice, or whole milk

1 tablespoon almond butter (or any nut or seed butter)

1/2 cup blueberries

2 tablespoons walnuts or pumpkin seeds, crushed or chopped

1 tablespoon flaxseeds, ground

1 tablespoon fresh coconut, shredded

1/2 banana, not too ripe, sliced

Optional: 1 tablespoon golden berries

FRITTATA

Serves 1 to 2, Vegetarian/Gluten-Free

INGREDIENTS

1 garlic clove, minced
1/4 cup onions, chopped
1 tablespoon olive oil, or Ziggy
  Marley's Coco'Mon Coconut Oil,
  or coconut oil of your choosing
1/2 cup freshly chopped tomato
3/4 cup fresh spinach, torn into
  large pieces
3 whole eggs, plus 2 egg whites
  (or egg substitute of your choosing)
1/4 cup whole milk
1/4 teaspoon sea salt
1/4 teaspoon freshly ground pepper
1/3 cup finely chopped basil leaves
1/2 cup feta cheese

APPLE CIDER DRESSING

Apple cider vinegar, like Bragg
  Apple Cider Vinegar
Olive oil
Salt and pepper, to taste
Optional: add minced garlic and
  shallots

or SIMPLE LEMON DRESSING

1 lemon, juiced
3 cloves garlic, minced
4–5 tablespoons of extra-virgin
  olive oil
Salt and pepper, to taste
Pinch of red pepper flakes

PREPARATION

Preheat oven to 350°F.

In a cast-iron skillet, sauté garlic and onions in olive oil or coconut oil until onion is soft.

Add tomatoes and spinach, allowing spinach to wilt.

In a large bowl, whisk eggs, egg whites, milk, salt, and pepper together.

After whisking, add egg mixture and chopped basil to the pan.

Sprinkle with feta cheese.

When edges of frittata start to firm against pan, remove from stovetop and place in oven until fully cooked, about 10 minutes.

Serve with side salad and apple cider vinaigrette or simple lemon dressing.

For apple cider and simple lemon salad dressings, mix all ingredients and whisk until combined. For cider dressing, desired yield is 1 part vinegar to 2 parts olive oil.

Optional: you can also make individual servings in ramekins.

I like to drink juices and smoothies, something I can have at any time of day. My body is very sensitive to what goes inside of it, which might be one of the reasons I'm drawn to food that nourishes. The Almond Coconut Smoothie (page 30) is something that can help carry me through the day, and it also reminds me of my father, who used to drink lots of juices. It reminds me of when he would take me to soccer games at National Stadium. (He was a Boys' Town fan because he was from Trench Town, but we left Trench Town when I was very young, so my team ended up being Harbour View. National Stadium is also where my dad played the One Love Peace Concert in 1978, but that's a whole other story.)

Another favorite all-day drink for me is the Date and Kale Smoothie (page 30). At home we grow kale in our small garden, and food you grow yourself just tastes better. Even as a kid, I was conscious of my parents' relationship with food. In Rasta culture eating fresh is natural, with a lot of vegetables, a lot of food that can be picked right outside your door. So, many of the recipes in this section are vegetable-heavy, and almost all the ingredients can be grown in a small garden.

TURMERIC COOLER

INGREDIENTS

2 chunks fresh turmeric
1 bunch greens (kale, lettuce, or spinach)
3 whole carrots
1 cucumber
1/2 or 1 lemon, your preference
1/2 inch fresh ginger
1 medium Granny Smith apple
1/4 pineapple, diced

PREPARATION

Wash vegetables and fruit thoroughly.
Juice all ingredients in a juicer.

BEET QUENCHER

INGREDIENTS

1 medium red beet
3 whole carrots
1 orange
1/4 pineapple
1/2 red bell pepper
1/4 jalapeño, or to your spice preference

PREPARATION

Wash vegetables and fruit thoroughly.
Juice 1 orange by hand and set aside.
Juice all other ingredients in a juicer.
Add orange juice.
Stir and enjoy.

ALL GREEN

INGREDIENTS

1/2 cup spinach
1/2 head of romaine lettuce
1 bunch kale
2 medium Granny Smith apples
1 cucumber
1 celery stalk
1/2 lemon

PREPARATION

Wash vegetables and fruit thoroughly.
Juice all ingredients in a juicer.

"My body is very sensitive to what goes inside of it, which might be one of the reasons I'm drawn to food that nourishes."

All drink recipes below serve 1, and are Vegetarian/Gluten-Free

HEALING SHOT

INGREDIENTS
1 teaspoon honey
1 pinch cayenne pepper
1 fresh garlic clove, minced
Optional: 1 lemon, juiced

PREPARATION
Mix all ingredients together and shoot it!

COCO LOVE JUICE

INGREDIENTS
1 coconut
Pinch of sea salt, or to taste
Pinch of freshly ground pepper, or to taste
Pinch of cinnamon
Pinch of nutmeg
Agave sweetener, to taste

PREPARATION
Remove water and meat from coconut.
Place in blender.
Add remaining ingredients and blend together.

SPICED LADY

INGREDIENTS
1 chunk fresh turmeric
1/4 pineapple
1/2 lemon
1/2 cup alkaline water
Honey, to taste
Cayenne pepper, to taste

PREPARATION
Juice turmeric, pineapple, and lemon in a juicer.
Combine with additional ingredients.

ALMOND COCONUT SMOOTHIE

Serves 1, Vegetarian/Vegan/Gluten-Free

INGREDIENTS

1/2 cup almond milk
2 tablespoons almond butter
1/4 cup Ziggy Marley's Hemp Rules
    Hempseeds, or hempseeds of your
    choosing
1/4 cup raw almonds
6 tablespoons flaxseeds, ground
6 dates, pitted and chopped
1 cup coconut water
1/4 cup coconut meat
Agave sweetener (or honey), to taste
Handful of ice

PREPARATION

Mix all ingredients together in blender until smooth. If you find that the smoothie is too thick, add almond milk or coconut water to achieve desired consistency.

KK JUICE

Serves 1, Vegetarian/Vegan/Gluten-Free

INGREDIENTS

2 cups coconut water
1/4 cup chia seeds
1 or 2 fresh mint leaves
1/2 pineapple
1/2 cucumber

PREPARATION

Wash mint and cucumber.
Add chia seeds to coconut water and let sit. While chia seed and coconut water mixture is sitting, juice the remainder of ingredients in a juicer.
Once juiced, add to coconut water and mix all ingredients together.

DATE AND KALE SMOOTHIE

Serves 2, Vegetarian/Vegan/Gluten-Free

INGREDIENTS

4 cups kale
6 dates, pitted
4 cups coconut milk
2 teaspoons Ziggy Marley's Coco'Mon
    Coconut Oil, or coconut oil of your
    choosing
Handful of ice
Optional: 1 scoop/serving vanilla protein
    powder

PREPARATION

Wash and remove ribs from kale.
Combine all ingredients in high-powered blender.
Blend and enjoy.

"The Almond Coconut Smoothie is something that can help carry me through the day, and it also reminds me of my father, who used to drink lots of juices."

"At home we grow kale in our small garden, and food you grow yourself just tastes better. In Rasta culture eating fresh is natural, with a lot of vegetables, a lot of food that can be picked right outside your door."

HEMPSEED PESTO

Yields approximately 1 cup, Vegetarian/Vegan/Gluten-Free

INGREDIENTS

1/2 cup Ziggy Marley's Hemp Rules Hempseeds, or hempseeds of your choosing
3 cups fresh basil, stemmed
Cracked pepper, to taste
3 tablespoons lemon juice
3 garlic cloves
1/2 cup extra-virgin olive oil
1 tablespoon Ziggy Marley's Coco'Mon Coconut Oil, or extra-virgin olive oil

PREPARATION

Blend all ingredients together in a food processor.

PRESERVED LEMONS

Yields 5, Vegetarian/Vegan/Gluten-Free

INGREDIENTS

1/2 cup kosher salt
5 whole lemons, for preserving
4 lemons, juiced
1 large sterilized canning jar (large enough to hold 5 whole lemons)
Optional: add bay leaves, whole allspice, or peppercorns

PREPARATION

Place salt at bottom of jar.

Cut tops of lemons off, stuff them in the jar, compress them, and cover lemons in lemon juice.

Leave some room at the top of jar before sealing.

Let sit in dark area for about 30 days, gently shaking every few days.

Preserved Lemons can be used in the Whole Roasted Branzino (p. 66).

COCONUT RICE

Serves 3 to 4, Vegetarian/Vegan/Gluten-Free

INGREDIENTS

2 cups rice
2 cups coconut milk
1 cup water
2 tablespoons Ziggy Marley's Coco'Mon Coconut Oil, or coconut oil of your choosing
Salt, to taste

PREPARATION

Combine ingredients in a saucepan and bring to a boil. Cover, reduce heat, and simmer for about 20 minutes.

VEGAN ROASTED GARLIC TAHINI

Yields approximately 1/2 cup, Vegetarian/Vegan/Gluten-Free

INGREDIENTS

1 fresh garlic bulb
2 tablespoons Ziggy Marley's Coco'Mon Coconut Oil, or coconut oil of your choosing
1/4 cup olive oil
1/2 cup tahini, stirred well
1/3 cup fresh lemon juice
1/2 teaspoon smoked paprika
1/2 teaspoon sea salt, or to taste
Hot water to blend (if necessary)

PREPARATION

Preheat oven to 400°F.

Slice top off whole garlic bulb. Spread coconut oil and a little olive oil over the garlic bulb and wrap in foil.

Roast garlic until soft, about 30–40 minutes.

Squeeze garlic cloves out of shells, place in food processor with the rest of the ingredients, and blend.

PICKLED CUCUMBERS

Vegetarian/Vegan/Gluten-Free

INGREDIENTS

4 Persian cucumbers
Salt and ground pepper, fresh and to taste
1/4 teaspoon soy sauce: low-sodium, gluten-free, or Bragg Liquid Aminos
1/2 teaspoon raw agave sweetener
1/2 Scotch bonnet or habanero pepper, seeded and thinly sliced
4 tablespoons apple cider vinegar, like Bragg Apple Cider Vinegar

PREPARATION

Thinly slice cucumbers.

Mix together remainder of ingredients.

Add cucumbers and let sit for at least 20 minutes.

Pickled Cucumbers can be used in the Ahi Tuna Burgers (p. 62).

CARIBBEAN SALSA

Vegetarian/Vegan/Gluten-Free

INGREDIENTS

1 cup fresh, firm mango, diced
1 cup fresh pineapple, diced
Optional: 1 cup fresh, firm papaya, diced
1/4 cup fresh jalapeño, minced and seeded, or to taste
1/4 cup red onion, minced
3 tablespoons fresh lime juice
1/2 teaspoon salt, kosher or sea
1 tablespoon freshly chopped cilantro
1 cup firm Roma tomatoes, diced and seeded
1/4 cup cucumber, diced and seeded
Ziggy Marley's Hemp Rules Hempseeds, or hempseeds of your choosing

PREPARATION

Combine all ingredients in a bowl and generously sprinkle hempseeds before serving.

Enjoy with chips and fresh green salad.

Really and truly, a good lunch for me is something light, so most of the recipes in this section are soups and salads. When my family was living in Bull Bay in the 1970s, Saturday was soup day. Saturday was also cleaning day. We'd get the soup going and then we'd clean the house, and the aroma would fill the air as we cleaned. One big pot of soup.

Fish has also been a central staple of my diet. In Bull Bay you could run down to the beach, to the Rasta fishermen living there. My father knew them—it was a real community—so there was always fresh fish. Fresh fish come, you make a fire, you put a piece of zinc over it, and cook it right there on the metal. It's very natural, very sustainable eating. The Fish Soup recipe (page 43) comes from this period of my life. One of the things that makes the recipe special—after adding in spices like turmeric, ginger, garlic, along with scallion stalks, kale, and squash—is the cho cho, an edible plant also called chayote that was first discovered in Jamaica in the middle of the eighteenth century (though I'm sure it was eaten by people on the island for centuries before that).

Another midday recipe I love is my sister's Lentil Soup (page 47). Karen is a great cook and she makes fancy stuff sometimes. In this soup, she gets the balance between the thyme, the garlic, the sea salt, the Jamaican allspice berries, and all the other ingredients just right. Everybody got to try Karen's lentil soup.

MIDDAY

FALL QUINOA SALAD

Serves 2 to 4, Vegetarian/Vegan/Gluten-Free

INGREDIENTS

1 cup pomegranate seeds
2 cups cooked quinoa, drained and cooled
1/2 cup dried cranberries
1 large bunch cilantro, minced
1 large bunch of mint, minced
3 green onions, minced
1/2 cup fresh lemon juice
Salt and pepper, to taste

PREPARATION

Mix all ingredients together and serve chilled.

MIAMI APPLE AND FETA SALAD

Serves 2 to 4, Vegetarian/Gluten-Free

INGREDIENTS

2 cups romaine lettuce, torn
2 cups red leaf lettuce, torn
1 medium Fuji apple, chopped
1/2 cup dried cranberries
1 tomato, chopped
Optional: 1 red onion, chopped

DRESSING
3 tablespoons olive oil
1 1/2 tablespoons white wine vinegar
1/4 cup fresh lemon juice
1/8 teaspoon pepper
1/8 teaspoon sea salt

TOPPING
1/2 cup walnuts, halved
1 cup feta, crumbled

PREPARATION

In a large bowl, combine salad ingredients, add dressing, and toss.

Sprinkle walnuts and feta cheese on top.

FENNEL SALAD

Serves 2, Vegetarian/Vegan/Gluten-Free

INGREDIENTS

2 fennel bulbs
Kosher salt, to taste
Lemon juice, to taste
Extra-virgin olive oil, to taste

PREPARATION

Slice fennel, including green stems and fennel fronds.

Add kosher salt, lemon juice, and extra-virgin olive oil.

Taste and toss.

Serve cold.

SUMMER QUINOA SALAD

Serves 4, Vegetarian/Vegan/Gluten-Free

INGREDIENTS

1 1/2 cups quinoa
1/2 teaspoon Ziggy Marley's Coco'Mon Coconut Oil, or coconut oil of your choosing
1 teaspoon extra-virgin olive oil
3 cups low-sodium vegetable stock
Salt, to taste
1/2 teaspoon fresh pepper, ground
5 Persian cucumbers, chopped
1 large tomato, seeded, cored, and diced
1/2 teaspoon smoked paprika
1/2 onion, chopped
1 1/2 cups black beans, cooked and rinsed (if canned)
1 bunch fresh parsley, chopped

PREPARATION

Combine quinoa with coconut oil, olive oil, and stock in a saucepan. Add salt and pepper to taste.

Cook for approximately 12 minutes over medium heat, covered.

After quinoa is cooked, remove from heat, fluff with a fork, and let cool.

Add remaining ingredients and dress with cider vinaigrette.

APPLE CIDER VINAIGRETTE
1/4 cup apple cider vinegar, like Bragg Apple
  Cider Vinegar
1/2 cup olive oil
Salt and pepper, fresh and to taste
1/2 teaspoon raw agave sweetener

PREPARATION

Whisk together and serve.

"One of the things that makes this recipe special is the cho cho, an edible plant also called chayote that was first discovered in Jamaica in the middle of the eighteenth century (though I'm sure it was eaten by people on the island for centuries before that)."

FISH SOUP

Serves 4 to 6, Gluten-Free

PREPARATION

Remove fish heads and set aside.

Fillet fish and set flesh aside.

Place allspice, fish heads, and bones into a stockpot.

Add 4 cups vegetable stock and bring to a boil.

Strain stock, discarding heads and bones. Return stock to pot, add remaining 4 cups of stock, and bring to a boil.

Add (optional) green bananas, cho cho (chayote), butternut squash, and carrot, and bring to a rapid boil.

Add fresh thyme, onion, bell peppers, turmeric, ginger, garlic, scallion, and salt and black pepper, and then add greens.

Place whole Scotch bonnet or habanero pepper and fish fillets on top and simmer on medium-high heat till fish is flaky and vegetables are cooked. Time varies depending on the fish; keep an eye on it.

Stir in coconut oil when fish begins to flake, and simmer for about 5 more minutes, and you're good to go.

Optional additions: noodles and/or a squeeze of lemon.

INGREDIENTS

2 medium-sized whole fish of your choosing, or 4 small-sized whole fish

6 whole Jamaican allspice berries

8 cups vegetable stock, no sodium or low-sodium

Optional: 3 green bananas, sliced

2 cho cho (chayote), peeled and sliced

1 cup butternut squash, chopped

2 large carrots, sliced

2–3 sprigs fresh thyme

1 small onion, chopped

1/2 green bell pepper, chopped

1/2 red bell pepper, chopped

1 tablespoon fresh turmeric, grated

1 tablespoon fresh ginger, grated

3 garlic cloves, peeled

2 scallion stalks, chopped

Salt and pepper, to taste

1 cup greens, chopped (kale, spinach, or collard greens)

1 whole Scotch bonnet or habanero pepper

1–2 tablespoons Ziggy Marley's Coco'Mon Coconut Oil, or coconut oil of your choosing

Optional additions: noodles of your choosing and lemon

COCONUT CURRY SQUASH SOUP

Serves 4, Vegetarian/Vegan/Gluten-Free

INGREDIENTS

1 tablespoon olive oil
1 medium carrot, peeled and diced
5 cups buttercup squash, chopped
1 medium celery stalk, diced
    with leaves
1 medium sweet onion, diced
1/2 scallion stalk
1 large tomato, chopped and diced
1/4 tablespoon freshly chopped
    thyme
1/2 teaspoon ground Jamaican
    allspice
1 whole bay leaf
Pinch of cayenne pepper
1 teaspoon coriander, ground
1 tablespoon curry powder
3 garlic cloves, minced
1 teaspoon Ziggy Marley's
    Coco'Mon Original or Curry
    Coconut Oil, or coconut oil of
    your choosing
1 quart vegetable broth
1 cup coconut milk
Sea salt and ground pepper,
    to taste
Cilantro, fresh and to taste

PREPARATION

Heat olive oil in a large stockpot and sauté carrots, squash, celery, onion, and scallion stalk (unchopped), until softened, approximately 10–12 minutes.

Add tomatoes, fresh thyme, allspice, bay leaf, cayenne pepper, coriander, curry powder, garlic, and coconut oil. Gently stir everything together.

Add broth and coconut milk to the pot. When liquid comes to a slight boil, turn down the heat and let simmer until everything is cooked, approximately 30 minutes. Remove scallion stalk and bay leaf. (Chop scallion stalk for optional topping.)

Season with salt and pepper to taste.

Use a hand blender, blender, or food processor to puree soup to desired consistency. Garnish with chopped scallion or cilantro.

"We have been cooking with coconut for a long time in Jamaica. You'd get it from the people in the market who would boil it. It wasn't something you would buy in a store."

BUTTERNUT SQUASH AND LEEK SOUP

Serves 4 to 6, Vegetarian/Vegan/Gluten-Free

INGREDIENTS

1 leek, cleaned and chopped
1 butternut squash, skinned and diced
1 tablespoon Ziggy Marley's Coco'Mon Curry Coconut Oil, or coconut oil
  of your choosing
6 cups vegetable stock
Cumin, to taste
1 tablespoon liquid amino acids, like Bragg Liquid Aminos
Black pepper, freshly ground, to taste
Agave sweetener, to taste
Ziggy Marley's Hemp Rules Hempseeds, or hempseeds of your choosing
Chopped parsley for garnish

PREPARATION

In a large pot over medium heat, sauté leeks and squash in coconut oil for 6 minutes.

Add stock, cumin, liquid aminos, pepper, and agave.

Turn heat to high and bring to a boil. Once boiling, reduce heat and simmer for 40 minutes.

Remove pot from stove and let soup cool, then use blender to blend squash and leeks, leaving no chunks or pieces.

Return to pot and warm on low heat, adding additional aminos and agave to taste.

Serve in bowls with hempseeds and chopped parsley sprinkled on top.

LENTIL SOUP

Serves 4 to 6, Vegetarian/Vegan/Gluten-Free

INGREDIENTS

1 tablespoon olive oil
1 medium carrot, peeled and diced
1 medium celery stalk, diced with leaves
1/2 medium sweet onion, diced
1 1/2 scallion stalks
1 large tomato, chopped and diced
1 (15-ounce) can of whole tomatoes, drained and diced
1 teaspoon freshly chopped thyme
3 whole Jamaican allspice berries
1 bay leaf
1 1/4 cups lentils, rinsed
3 garlic cloves, minced
1 teaspoon Ziggy Marley's Coco'Mon Original or Curry Coconut Oil, or coconut oil
   of your choosing
1 quart vegetable broth
Sea salt and freshly ground pepper, to taste
1 teaspoon red wine vinegar
1/2 bunch kale, loosely chopped

PREPARATION

Heat olive oil in a large stockpot and sauté carrots, celery, onion, and whole scallions until softened, approximately 10–12 minutes.

Add tomatoes, fresh thyme, allspice berries, bay leaf, lentils, garlic, and coconut oil. Lightly stir everything together.

Add broth to the pot. When liquid comes to a slight boil, turn down heat and let simmer for about 30–40 minutes, until lentils are tender. Remove whole scallion.

Taste and season with salt and pepper if necessary.

Stir in vinegar and add kale, cook until wilted.

"In this soup recipe, my sister gets the balance between the thyme, the garlic, the sea salt, the Jamaican allspice berries, and all the other ingredients just right. Everybody got to try Karen's lentil soup."

TOFU IN COCONUT CARROT CURRY

Serves 6 to 8, Vegetarian/Vegan/
Gluten-Free

PREPARATION

Place all dry spices in spice or coffee grinder and grind to powder. Set aside.

Heat oil in medium pot and add vegetables. Stir constantly to soften, about 4 minutes.

Add spice mixture and toast, stirring constantly for 1 minute, scraping bottom to prevent sticking.

Add stock, carrot juice, and coconut milk. (Be sure to reserve the heavier "cream" of the coconut milk for later use.)

Bring to boil, and then simmer about 45–60 minutes until liquid reduced by 2/3.

Strain through a fine-meshed sieve or strainer into a smaller, clean pot.

Add tofu (or other protein), gently bring to boil.

Finish by whisking in reserved coconut cream and season to taste.

Serve over rice or other grain.

INGREDIENTS

2 tablespoons coriander seed
1 tablespoon plus 1 teaspoon
    cinnamon
1 tablespoon fennel seed
1 teaspoon turmeric
1 teaspoon black peppercorns
3 star anise
2 cloves
1 teaspoon salt
2 carrots, peeled and sliced
1 rib celery, diced
1 medium onion, finely sliced
3 ounces fresh ginger, peeled
    and finely julienned
1 fresh jalapeño, sliced lengthwise
2 cups chicken stock, vegetable
    stock, or water
2 cups fresh carrot juice
1 (13.5-ounce) can coconut milk,
    refrigerated, then separate
    "cream" from milk
2 pounds extra-firm tofu, cut into
    quarters (use plain tofu for
    gluten-free recipe)
Rice or cooked grain, 1 cooked cup
    per serving

Dinner is the most enjoyable meal in my family: eating, talking, hearing about each other's day. It was the same when I was growing up, so we kick off this section with a classic Jamaican recipe, Jerk Chicken (page 52). In truth, although chicken was a popular dinner dish in my childhood, I didn't start coming to eat jerk chicken until I was a teenager. This recipe will taste best if you use Scotch bonnet peppers.

Wild Red Snapper (page 55) is also very Jamaican, especially how it works with okra. A lot of us who grew up there love the food that has been passed on in stories as much as the plate. According to Jamaican folklore, okra makes you strong, more manly, more virile. Plus, Jamaica has the best okra I ever tasted. The other okra-based recipe we have here is the Whole Roasted Branzino (page 66), with a different twist: you caramelize the okra.

One of my favorite creations is the Coconut Dream Fish (page 58). We have been cooking with coconut for a long time in Jamaica. You'd get it from the people in the market who would boil it. It wasn't something you would buy in a store. The Coconut Dream Fish is a take on the traditional Jamaican brown stew fish. You fry the sea bass lightly with coconut oil, then cook it down with onion, garlic, and other seasoning. Real herbs and spices from the earth give the best flavor. And then you add the coconut milk, so the whole thing have this deep coconutiness. When I first made it I thought, *Oh, this is like a coconut dream!* Makes you go to bed real nice.

JERK CHICKEN

Serves 4 to 6, Gluten-Free

INGREDIENTS

1 whole chicken, separated into pieces
2 Scotch bonnet peppers, seeds removed
1 tablespoon salt, or to taste
1 teaspoon black pepper, freshly ground
1 teaspoon allspice
1 teaspoon nutmeg
4 garlic cloves
1 1/2 teaspoons thyme, dried
1 teaspoon fresh thyme
1/2 cup scallions, chopped
1 tablespoon Ziggy Marley's Coco'Mon Coconut Oil, or coconut oil of your choosing
1 lemon, sliced into 4–6 pieces

PREPARATION

Set chicken aside.

Using a food processor, blend remaining ingredients into a paste (except for the lemon slices).

Rub all over chicken.

Grill chicken over medium or medium-high heat for 5–6 minutes on each side, or until thoroughly cooked.

Serve with lemon slices.

"Although chicken was a popular dinner dish in my childhood, I didn't start coming to eat jerk chicken until I was a teenager."

"Red snapper is also very Jamaican, especially how it works with okra. According to Jamaican folklore, okra makes you strong, more manly, more virile. Plus, Jamaica has the best okra I ever tasted."

WILD RED SNAPPER

Serves 4

PREPARATION

Season fish with salt and pepper.

Spread flour on a plate large enough to fit fish.

Heat 2 tablespoons oil in pan at high heat. Dredge fish with flour and fry until nice and brown, approximately 5 minutes per side. Set aside.

In a large pot, add onions and bell peppers, and sauté over medium heat until onions are translucent, approximately 10–12 minutes.

Add remaining ingredients (not including the plantains) and simmer over low heat for about 5 minutes, or until liquid is reduced almost completely.

Meanwhile, fry plantains with remaining 2 tablespoons of olive oil, set aside.

Plate all vegetables on a large platter, layer fish and fried plantains. Serve immediately.

INGREDIENTS

2 whole red snappers (1 1/2 pounds each)
Salt and pepper, to taste
1/2 cup all-purpose flour
4 tablespoons olive oil
1/2 yellow onion, chopped
1/2 red bell pepper, chopped
1/2 green bell pepper, chopped
1/2 orange bell pepper, chopped
1/2 yellow bell pepper, chopped
3 garlic cloves, thinly sliced
2 sprigs fresh thyme
1 cup fresh tomato, chopped
20 pieces okra, sliced
1/4 cup coconut milk
1/4 cup water
2 ripe plantains, sliced

JAMAICAN RICE AND PEAS

Serves 4, Vegetarian/Vegan/Gluten-Free

INGREDIENTS

2 cans (15.5 ounces per can) medium-sized red kidney beans
1 can (15.5 ounces) coconut milk
Water
1 small onion, chopped
1 garlic clove, chopped
1/4 teaspoon thyme, dried
2 tablespoons Ziggy Marley's Coco'Mon Original, Lemon-Ginger Coconut Oil,
   or coconut oil of your choosing
2 cups rice
1 Scotch bonnet pepper, left whole

PREPARATION

Drain liquid from beans into a measuring cup and add coconut milk with enough water to make 4 cups of liquid.

Pour liquid into a saucepan with beans, onion, garlic, thyme, and oil. Bring to a boil.

Add rice and stir for 1 minute. Reduce heat to medium-low.

Place Scotch bonnet pepper on top of liquid and cook, covered, for 30 minutes or until rice is tender.

Remove Scotch bonnet before serving.

HUACHINANGO À LA VERACRUZANA

Serves 4, Gluten-Free

INGREDIENTS

4 red snapper fillets (6 ounces each)
4 pieces parchment paper, big enough to wrap fillets
2 tablespoons olive oil
1 medium white onion, julienned
1 large red bell pepper, julienned
1 large green bell pepper, julienned
2 medium tomatoes, peeled and diced
1 ounce white wine
Salt and pepper, to taste
24 caper berries
2 tablespoons freshly chopped cilantro
12 green olives, pitted and quartered
1/4 cup fresh lemon juice
Rice, 1 cooked cup per serving

PREPARATION

Preheat oven to 450°F.

Heat a large sauté pan on medium. Add olive oil, then onions and peppers, and cook for 2 minutes.

Add tomatoes, sauté for 30 seconds, and quickly add white wine. Cook another 30 seconds and season with salt and pepper to taste.

Remove pan from heat. Add capers, cilantro, olives, and lemon juice.

In a 12-inch sheet pan, place each fillet on a piece of parchment paper, topping with sautéed mixture. Wrap parchment paper around fish, and bake for 10 minutes.

Remove from oven and serve with rice.

COCONUT DREAM FISH

Serves 4, Gluten-Free

INGREDIENTS

4 fillets wild sea bass
Salt, to taste
1/2 teaspoon lemon pepper
4–6 tablespoons Ziggy Marley's
    Coco'Mon Coconut Oil, or
    coconut oil of your choosing
1/2 cup vegetable stock
1 medium onion, chopped
2 medium bell peppers
3 whole garlic cloves
1 teaspoon fresh ginger, grated
2–3 sprigs fresh thyme (some
    chopped for garnish)
6 whole Jamaican allspice berries
1/2 teaspoon cayenne pepper
1/2 teaspoon curry powder
1/2 cup coconut milk
Lime, quartered, for garnish

PREPARATION

Season fish fillets with salt and lemon pepper in the same skillet you will cook with.

Rub 1 tablespoon coconut oil onto seasoned fish, massaging for a few minutes. You've reached stage one of coconutiness. Remove fillets from pan and set aside.

Warm remaining coconut oil in the skillet over medium heat until oil is hot.

Return fillets to pan and fry on each side for 3–5 minutes, until slightly browned.

Remove fillets and place in a dish. You've reached stage two of coconutiness.

Add 4 tablespoons vegetable stock to the same skillet and scrape all the fish goodness from the bottom, deglazing the skillet and stirring. Lower heat if necessary, so as to not burn.

Add onions, bell pepper, garlic, ginger, thyme, allspice, cayenne pepper, and curry powder, and stir until mixture starts bubbling (about a minute or so).

Stir in coconut milk, remainder of vegetable stock, and heat 2–3 minutes until it comes to a boil, then reduce heat.

Lay fish fillets back in the pan and simmer for a few minutes, just so the fish can incorporate all the sauce. Try to make sure the fillets are kept whole.

Turn off heat, garnish with fresh chopped thyme and lime wedges, and serve on a platter, family style. You've reached the final stage of coconutiness.

This dish is gingery and coconutty with a hint of curry and a little spice. It tastes clean and will leave you feeling well-fed but not full—Jamaican style.

"This recipe has a deep coconutiness. When I first made it I thought, Oh, this is like a coconut dream! Makes you go to bed real nice."

ROASTED CAULIFLOWER

Serves 2 to 4, Vegetarian/Vegan/Gluten-Free

PREPARATION

Preheat oven to 375°F.

On a roasting pan, lay out the floret slices and drizzle with olive oil.

Season cauliflower with pepper, salt, paprika, cumin, curry powder, minced garlic, and coconut oil.

Roast in oven for about 40 minutes or until golden brown.

Roasted Cauliflower can be used in the Brown Rice and Salmon Bowl (p. 78).

INGREDIENTS

1 head cauliflower, washed, cut
  into florets, and sliced
1 clove garlic, minced
*Sea salt and black pepper, freshly
  ground
*1 tablespoon smoked paprika
*1 tablespoon cumin
*1 tablespoon curry powder
*1 tablespoon olive oil
*1 tablespoon Ziggy Marley's
  Coco'Mon Curry Coconut Oil, or
  coconut oil of your choosing

Adjust to your seasoning preference

AHI TUNA BURGERS

Serves 4, Gluten-Free

INGREDIENTS

1 1/2 pounds ahi tuna
2 teaspoons freshly grated ginger
1 garlic clove, smashed and minced
1 tablespoon fish sauce
1/4 cup onions, chopped
1 tablespoon fresh Thai basil, chopped
1 tablespoon fresh cilantro, chopped
1 1/2 teaspoons sesame oil
Brioche or buns of your choosing: gluten-free, pretzel buns, etc.
Pickled cucumbers (see recipe, p. 35)
4–8 leaves butter lettuce
2 heirloom tomatoes, sliced

PREPARATION

Finely chop tuna and combine with ginger, garlic, fish sauce, onions, Thai basil, cilantro, and sesame oil.

Form 4 patties, cover in plastic wrap, and chill in refrigerator for at least 30 minutes.

Grill burgers to liking and serve on brioche/buns with pickled cucumbers, butter lettuce, and heirloom tomatoes.

SWEET POTATO OVEN FRIES

Serves 2 to 4, Vegetarian/Vegan/ Gluten-Free

PREPARATION

Preheat oven to 425°F.

Slice potatoes in half lengthwise, then slice into wedges and place on baking sheet.

Drizzle lightly with coconut oil and sprinkle with salt and cumin.

Bake for 50 minutes, flipping after 30 minutes.

Remove once wedges are tender, slightly crispy on the outside, and golden brown.

INGREDIENTS

1 pound sweet potatoes
2 tablespoons Ziggy Marley's Coco'Mon Curry Coconut Oil, or coconut oil of your choosing
Salt, to taste
Cumin, to taste

WHOLE ROASTED BRANZINO

WITH CARAMELIZED OKRA AND PRESERVED LEMON

Serves 4 to 6, Gluten-Free

INGREDIENTS

2 whole branzino, cleaned and
  gutted
3 tablespoons olive oil
1 teaspoon Ziggy Marley's
  Coco'Mon Coconut Oil, or
  coconut oil of your choosing
3/4 cup okra, chopped
3 fresh garlic cloves, minced
6 fresh garlic cloves, whole
1 sprig fresh thyme, finely chopped
6 sprigs fresh thyme
1/2 teaspoon salt
1/2 teaspoon freshly ground pepper
1 preserved lemon, chopped
  (see recipe, p. 32)
1 freshly sliced lemon
1 cup cherry tomatoes
Optional: add 1/4 cup cooking
  wine halfway through roasting
3 tablespoons fresh parsley,
  chopped

PREPARATION

Preheat oven to 400°F.

In a baking pan combine 2 tablespoons olive oil, 1 teaspoon coconut oil, and okra.

Bake approximately 3–5 minutes, until okra turns a little brown, gently shaking pan to avoid burning.

When done, remove okra from pan.

With a mortar and pestle, combine minced garlic, chopped thyme, salt, and pepper, and mash until achieving the consistency of a rub.

Dress fish by rubbing 1 tablespoon of olive oil and the spice mixture all over the outside and inside.

Place 1/4 of preserved lemon in cavity of each fish with sprigs of fresh thyme, a few slices of fresh lemon, and whole garlic cloves.

Slice remaining preserved lemon and place atop each fish, along with the rest of the fresh lemon slices. Place in oven and cook in the same baking pan for approximately 20 minutes.

Halfway through cooking the fish, add cherry tomatoes (and optional cooking wine).

After fish is fully cooked, remove from oven and sprinkle with fresh parsley.

ESCABECHE

Serves 4, Gluten-Free

INGREDIENTS

1 pound white fish, skin on, and cut into 2-ounce pieces
White vinegar and 1/4 cup fresh lime juice or lemon juice, for washing fish
1 small red bell pepper, sliced thin
1 sweet onion, peeled, halved, and thinly sliced
5 garlic cloves, sliced thin
Zest of 1 Meyer lemon
1/4 cup Meyer lemon juice
1/4 cup rice vinegar
2 tablespoons sugar
2 sprigs thyme, leaves removed from stem
Olive oil, to taste
Sea salt, to taste

PREPARATION

Wash fish thoroughly in generous amounts of white vinegar and lemon or lime juice, pat dry with paper towels.

Combine bell pepper, onions, garlic, lemon zest and juice, rice vinegar, sugar, and thyme in a bowl and stir.

Place each piece of fish on a cedar plank (or a baking dish or plate). Torch skin (or panfry before, skin side down) for 1 minute a side, at most, until crispy and fish is 60–70% cooked. Move warm fish to a shallow, nonreactive container (such as a Pyrex baking dish), and pour vegetables and marinade evenly over fish.

Season with drizzled olive oil and sea salt to taste, and serve with salad or crusty bread.

COCONUT ESCABECHE

Serves 4, Gluten-Free

INGREDIENTS

1 pound white fish, thinly sliced
1/4 cup Ziggy Marley's Coco'Mon
    Lemon-Ginger Coconut Oil, or
    coconut oil of your choosing
1 cup coconut milk
1 stalk lemongrass
4 Kaffir lime leaves
2 serrano chilies
2 Fresno chilies
1 lime, juiced
Sea salt or sea salt flakes

PREPARATION

Slowly warm coconut oil in pan until it is just above room temperature (approximately 70°F).

Remove from heat and add slices of fish. Warm fish through without cooking or changing its appearance. Let marinate 15 minutes.

While fish is marinating, pour coconut milk into saucepan with lemongrass, Kaffir lime leaves, and chilies. Simmer sauce on medium heat.

When fish is ready, strain coconut milk. Arrange fillets on serving platter and add a small amount of sauce to each piece. Finish with a splash of lime juice and pinch of sea salt, and serve.

"Fish is a central staple of my diet. In Bull Bay you could run down to the beach, to the Rasta fishermen living there. My father knew them—it was a real community—so there was always fresh fish. Fresh fish come, you make a fire, you put a piece of zinc over it, and cook it right there on the metal. It's very natural, very sustainable eating."

CURRY ESCOVITCH

Serves 4

PREPARATION

Clean fish with juice of 1 lime and score skin a few times.

Season fish inside and out with salt and pepper.

Place seasoned flour in a shallow plate, and dredge each fish in flour, shaking to remove excess.

Pour coconut oil into a large cast-iron skillet until 1/4-inch deep, and cook on medium heat until hot. (Cast-iron skillets sometimes run hot, so you might need to reduce the stovetop temperature slightly.)

Fry 8 garlic cloves in coconut oil until golden brown, remove and reserve.

Add fish to pan and fry 3–4 minutes on each side until brown and crisp. Place warm fish in a shallow nonreactive container (such as a Pyrex baking dish), and set aside.

Add the 2 sliced garlic cloves to coconut oil and cook, stirring, until golden brown, about 1 minute.

Add bay leaves, allspice, sugar, chilies, carrots, cho cho (chayote), and shallots, and cook, stirring, until softened, about 2–3 minutes.

Add vinegar and bring to a boil; cook for 2 minutes.

Pour sauce over fish and let sit at room temperature for 1 hour before serving. Garnish with lime and fried garlic cloves, and serve with fried sweet potato chips or bammy (a traditional Jamaican flatbread).

INGREDIENTS

3 pounds small whole fish, cleaned and gutted (preferably red snapper, substitute 4 fillets if necessary)

3 limes (1 to wash fish, 2 for garnish)

Salt and pepper to season fish

1 cup flour, seasoned with salt and pepper

Ziggy Marley's Coco'Mon Curry Coconut Oil, or coconut oil of your choosing

10 garlic cloves (8 whole, 2 sliced)

2 bay leaves

6–8 Jamaican allspice berries

1 teaspoon sugar

5–6 Fresno chilies, thinly sliced into circles

2–3 serrano chilies, thinly sliced into circles

1–2 carrots, julienned

1–2 cho cho (chayote), julienned

3 large shallots, thinly sliced

1/2 cup white vinegar

Fried sweet potato chips or bammy

ROASTED YAM TART

Serves 2 to 4, Vegetarian

INGREDIENTS

1 puff pastry sheet
1/2 pound yams, sliced
1/2 cup onion, sliced
1 teaspoon fresh thyme
1 tablespoon Ziggy Marley's
   Coco'Mon Coconut Oil, or
   coconut oil of your choosing
1/2 teaspoon salt
1/4 teaspoon freshly ground pepper
2 tablespoons olive oil
1/2 cup feta, crumbled
Hempseeds, as desired

PREPARATION

Preheat oven to 375°F. Parbake the puff pastry sheet on a sheet pan to 80% of package cooking time.

At the same time, combine the yams, onions, thyme, 1/2 tablespoon coconut oil, salt, pepper, and 1 1/2 tablespoons olive oil on a sheet pan and roast alongside puff pastry.

When pastry sheet is parbaked, remove from oven and brush with 1/2 tablespoon of each oil.

Remove vegetable filling from oven, making sure the yams are soft, and spread evenly over pastry.

Top with feta cheese and hempseeds, and bake until the cheese somewhat melts and puff pastry cooking time is complete (i.e., the final 20% of the package cooking time).

Garnish with fresh thyme.

VEGETARIAN HASH

Serves 4, Vegetarian/Gluten-Free

PREPARATION

Slice potato, apple, carrot, onion, zucchini, cabbage, and pepper to the thickness of a quarter.

Heat olive oil in a large sauté pan and cook potatoes, apple, carrots, and onions for 2 minutes.

Add zucchinis, red cabbage, corn kernels, red pepper, and green peas. Cook for another 2 minutes, then add spinach and salt and pepper to taste. Divide evenly on 4 plates.

To poach egg whites: Add white vinegar and salt to a pot of water; bring to a simmer. Slide egg whites into pot slowly. Poach until opaque, about 2 minutes. With a slotted spoon, plate 2 eggs on top of each dish of hash.

Add salt and pepper to taste.

INGREDIENTS

2 tablespoons olive oil
1 small red potato
1/2 small red apple
1/2 medium-sized carrot
1/4 small white onion
1/2 small green zucchini
1/2 small yellow zucchini
1 small wedge red cabbage
1 tablespoon fresh corn kernels
1/2 red bell pepper
1 tablespoon fresh green peas
1/2 pound baby spinach, washed
Salt and pepper, to taste
1 ounce white vinegar
8 egg whites (2 per person)

BROWN RICE & SALMON BOWL

Serves 3 to 4, Gluten-Free

INGREDIENTS

1 salmon fillet (1 pound)

1 head cauliflower, florets quartered, cut into bite-size pieces (*or see recipe for Roasted Cauliflower, p. 61*)

1 whole leek (discard outer layer, then clean and slice)

Olive oil for drizzling, plus 1 tablespoon for sautéing

Salt and pepper, to taste

Cumin, to taste

1 bunch beet greens, julienned, stems removed

1 clove garlic, minced

2 tablespoons Ziggy Marley's Coco'Mon Lemon-Ginger Coconut Oil, or coconut oil of your choosing

3 cups cooked brown rice

1/2 avocado

PREPARATION

Preheat oven to 375°F.

Spread cauliflower and leeks on roasting pan, drizzle with olive oil, salt, pepper, and cumin.

Roast for 40 minutes, loosening cauliflower with wooden spoon halfway through to prevent sticking.

Salt salmon, divide into 3 pieces, set aside.

Sauté beet greens in olive oil, adding minced garlic.

Cook salmon in a frying pan with coconut oil until pink in the middle.

Scoop cooked brown rice into bowl, cover with roasted cauliflower and leeks.

Place salmon and beet greens on top.

Open avocado and slice lengthwise into pieces for garnish.

JAMAICAN DUMPLINGS

Yield varies, based on your preferred dumpling size, Vegetarian

INGREDIENTS

4 cups all-purpose flour
2 teaspoons baking powder
1 1/2 teaspoons salt
1 tablespoon butter
1/2 cup cold water
Olive oil, vegetable oil, or grape-seed oil for frying, enough to fill skillet halfway

PREPARATION

Combine dry ingredients in a large bowl. Then, stir in butter until flour mixture is in crumbles no larger than peas.

Mix in water 1 tablespoon at a time, just until the mixture is wet enough to form into a ball. The dough should have a firm consistency. Knead briefly and let rest for 5–10 minutes.

Heat oil in a large, heavy skillet over medium heat until hot. Break off pieces of dough and shape into patties—similar to flat biscuits.

Place just enough of the dumplings in the pan so they are not crowded.

Fry on each side until golden brown, about 3 minutes per side.

Remove from pan and drain on paper towels before serving.

ROAST CHICKEN

Serves 4 to 6

INGREDIENTS

1 roasting chicken (5–6 pounds)
1/4 cup fresh lemon juice
Kosher salt and freshly ground black pepper, to taste
2 tablespoons smoked paprika
1 tablespoon Herbes de Provence
1 head garlic, cut in half crosswise, plus 2 cloves minced
1 lemon, zested (approximately 1 tablespoon) and halved
2 teaspoons Ziggy Marley's Coco'Mon Coconut Oil, or coconut oil of your choosing
3 tablespoons extra-virgin olive oil
1 large bunch fresh thyme
1/2 cup chicken stock
1 large yellow onion, thickly sliced

PREPARATION

Preheat oven to 400°F.

Remove giblets and rinse chicken inside out with water and lemon juice.

Trim fat, remove feathers if necessary, and pat dry.

With a mortar and pestle, combine salt, pepper, smoked paprika, Herbes de Provence, 2 cloves minced garlic, and lemon zest. Once combined, add oils and mix to form a rub.

Season chicken with salt and pepper on the inside and stuff cavity with thyme, remainder of lemon, and garlic head.

Rub 3/4 of oil and herb mixture on outside of chicken. Tie legs together with kitchen string and tuck wingtips under the body.

Spread the balance of oil and herb mixture on bottom of roasting pan, adding in stock and onions.

Place chicken directly on top of mixture in roasting pan and cook for 90 minutes or until juices run clear. (An instant-read thermometer can be helpful. If used, make sure it's inserted into the thickest part of the chicken—chicken is cooked when the internal temperature reaches 165°F.)

Remove chicken, place on a platter, and let rest, covered with aluminum foil, for approximately 20 minutes, then serve.

FALAFEL AND HUMMUS

Serves 4 to 6, Vegetarian

PREPARATION

FALAFEL

Soak beans for 48 hours with hot water and 1 teaspoon baking powder. Change water at least twice.

In a food processor, blend beans with garlic, onion, cilantro, parsley, black pepper, salt, and cumin. Make into balls approximately the size of golf balls.

Heat oil in a large, heavy skillet over medium heat until hot.

Place just enough of the balls in the pan so they are not crowded. Fry for approximately 6–8 minutes total, turning the falafel regularly, until all the falafel balls have an even golden-brown color.

Remove from skillet and drain on paper towels before serving.

Pair with hummus, tahini, and your favorite salad, with the option to serve in pita bread, sandwich style.

HUMMUS

Combine garbanzo beans, garlic, tahini, lemon juice, water, salt, and pepper in food processor. Mix until soft and white. Stir in mayonnaise (optional).

Serve cold with a drizzle of olive oil, paprika, and pine nuts.

INGREDIENTS

FALAFEL

2 cups dry garbanzo beans
1 teaspoon baking powder
Water, enough to cover beans while soaking overnight
1 head garlic
1 large white onion
1 cup cilantro
1 cup parsley
1 teaspoon black pepper, freshly ground
1 teaspoon salt
2 teaspoons cumin
Vegetable oil, enough to fill 1/2 inch of a frying pan

HUMMUS

1 can garbanzo beans, washed with hot water
2 heads garlic
6 ounces tahini paste
1/2 cup fresh lemon juice
1 cup warm water
1/2 teaspoon salt
1/2 teaspoon pepper
1 teaspoon mayonnaise (optional)
Olive oil, to drizzle
Paprika, to taste
Pine nuts, for garnish

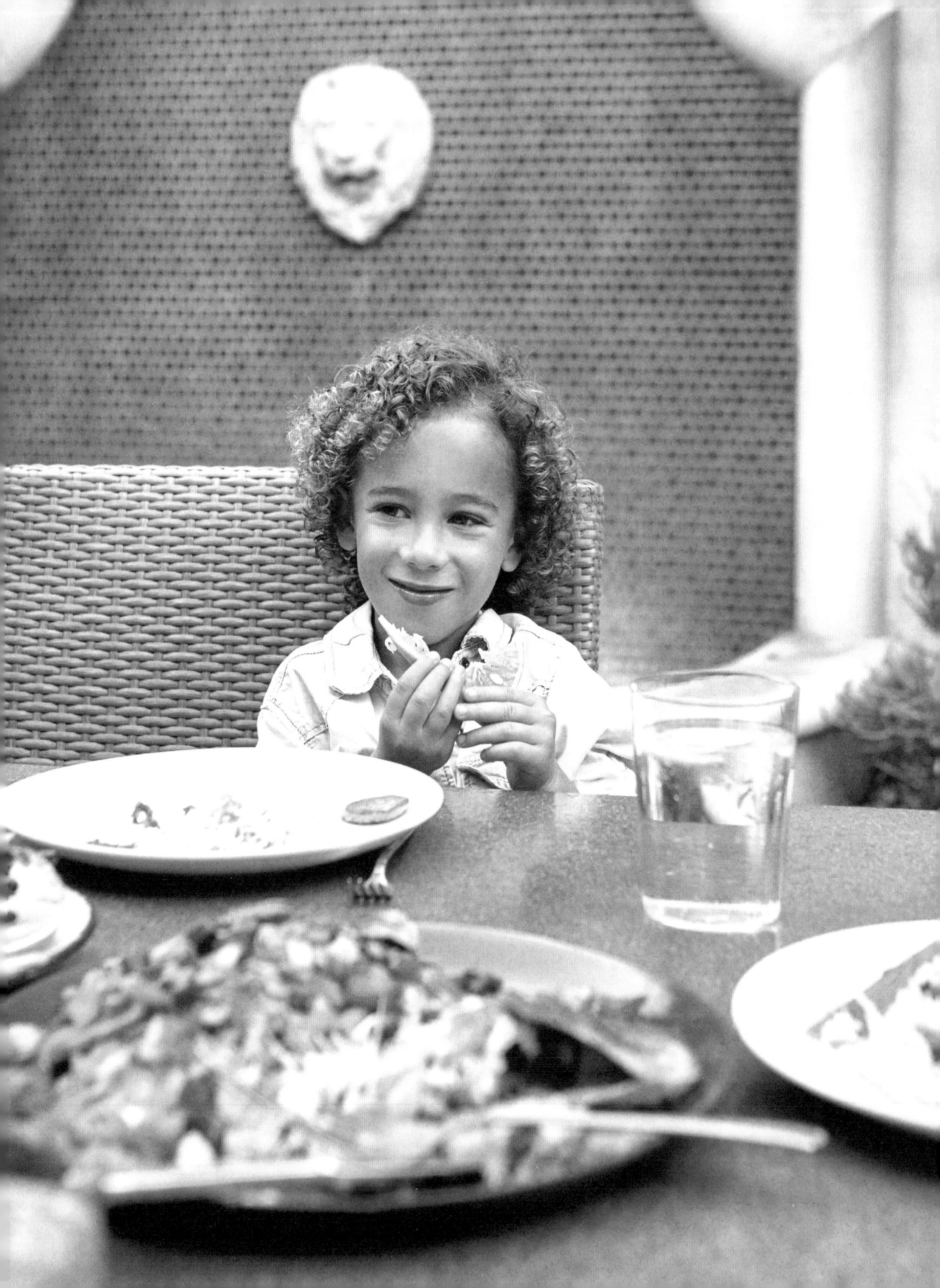

Many sweets—including the Stout Gingerbread (page 86), the Chocolate Chip Cookies (page 89), and Mamá Carmelita's Flan (page 93)—remind me of the incredible baking my auntie would do for birthday parties when I was growing up. Birthdays were when you killed the goat and cooked it in a big fire outside, a giant pot, making curry goat, mannish water, because the party wasn't just for the children, it was for the community. But then auntie brought out the cakes and other sweets she had baked. Talk about coconutiness.

I think my favorite is the Stout Gingerbread. One cup of Guinness helps make it delicious. A stout has more of the hops and B vitamins than a regular beer. It's important to get those vitamins in there, you know? That's what the Guinness is for, because I don't have no real need to drink beer. My body does not ask me for beer. Alcohol in general, I'm not curious or nothing. My culture is very deeply embedded in me, and we don't believe in alcohol so much.

But when the gingerbread is asking for the stout, that's another story. Sometimes the stories food tells are the best.

STOUT GINGER-BREAD

Yields 1 loaf, Vegetarian

INGREDIENTS

1 1/4 sticks of butter, or substitute
  1 teaspoon Ziggy Marley's
  Coco'Mon Coconut Oil
1 cup (packed) dark brown sugar
1 cup stout beer, like Guinness
3 teaspoons ground ginger
1 tablespoon fresh ginger, peeled
  and grated
2 teaspoons cinnamon
1/4 teaspoon cloves, ground
1/2 cup molasses
1/2 cup golden syrup
2 cups all-purpose flour
2 teaspoons baking soda
2 eggs
1 1/4 cups sour cream

PREPARATION

Preheat oven to 325°F.

On low heat, mix the following in a saucepan: butter, sugar, stout, ground ginger, fresh ginger, cinnamon, ground cloves, molasses, and golden syrup.

Remove from heat and whisk in flour and baking soda till lumps have disappeared.

In a bowl, whisk eggs and sour cream.

Add egg mixture to the gingerbread mixture and whisk till smooth.

Add mixture to a greased loaf pan and bake for about 45 minutes, testing with a toothpick at 35 minutes for doneness.

"A stout has more of the hops and B vitamins than a regular beer. It's important to get those vitamins in there, you know? That's what the Guinness is for, because I don't have no real need to drink beer. My body does not ask me for beer. But when the gingerbread is asking for the stout, that's another story."

CINNAMON ORANGE ALMOND POPCORN

Serves 4 to 6, Vegetarian/Vegan/Gluten-Free

INGREDIENTS

1/2 cup popcorn kernels
2 tablespoons Ziggy Marley's Coco'Mon Orange-Almond Coconut Oil, or coconut oil
  of your choosing
1/4 cup agave sweetener
2 teaspoons cinnamon
1/4 teaspoon sea salt

PREPARATION

Pop popcorn and put into a large bowl.

Melt coconut oil over low heat. Add agave sweetener, cinnamon, and salt, and stir well.

Pour mixture over popcorn and stir well to combine.

Serve.

DATE BAR

Yield varies, based on your preferred bar size, Vegetarian/Vegan/Gluten-Free

INGREDIENTS

1/4 cup almonds
1/4 cup walnuts (or any nut you prefer)
1/2 cup dates, pitted
1/3 cup Ziggy Marley Hemp Rules Hempseeds, or hempseeds of your choosing
1/2 cup coconut, dry and grated
1 teaspoon cinnamon
2 tablespoons Ziggy Marley's Coco'Mon Coconut Oil, or coconut oil of your choosing

PREPARATION

Place everything into a food processor and lightly chop.

Remove mixture and form into individual bars or roll into balls.

CHOCOLATE CHIP COOKIES

Yields approximately 2 dozen cookies, Vegetarian/Gluten-Free

INGREDIENTS

1/4 cup Ziggy Marley's Coco'Mon Original or Orange-Almond Coconut Oil, or coconut oil of your choosing

1 cup whole wheat pastry flour or all-purpose gluten-free flour

2/3 cup organic sugar

1 teaspoon baking powder

1/4 teaspoon sea salt

2 tablespoons nondairy milk (rice milk, almond milk, or hemp milk)

2 teaspoons vanilla extract

1/2 cup chocolate chips (milk or dark chocolate; or dairy-free chocolate can be used as a vegan substitute)

PREPARATION

Preheat your oven to 350°F.

Melt coconut oil over low heat.

Combine flour, sugar, baking powder, and salt in a bowl, and stir well.

Mix melted coconut oil, nondairy milk, and vanilla, and stir into the dry mixture just until thoroughly combined. Stir in chocolate chips.

Scoop the mixture in tablespoon increments onto 2 lightly oiled cookie sheets.

Bake for about 10 minutes or until very lightly browned. You want them to almost look underdone or they won't be as soft.

Remove to a cooling rack and serve when cooled.

"This reminds me of the incredible baking my auntie would do for birthday parties when I was growing up. The party wasn't just for the children, it was for the community."

ORANGE ALMOND CHOCOLATE TRUFFLES

Yields approximately 16 truffles,
Vegetarian/Vegan/Gluten-Free

PREPARATION

In a food processor, blend all ingredients (except for
2 teaspoons of cacao powder) until well combined.
Alternatively, you can mix this with a whisk by hand, as long
as mixture is completely smooth.

Place in the freezer for about 20 minutes, or until mixture can
be shaped into balls.

Form into tablespoon-sized balls and dust with 2 teaspoons
of cacao powder.

Stored in an airtight container in the fridge, truffles will keep
for at least 2 weeks.

INGREDIENTS

1/2 cup raw cacao powder, plus
    additional 2 teaspoons for dusting
1/4 cup Ziggy Marley's Coco'Mon
    Orange-Almond Coconut Oil, or
    coconut oil of your choosing
1/4 cup raw agave sweetener
1 tablespoon vanilla
1/4 teaspoon sea salt

MAMÁ CARMELITA'S FLAN

(EGG CUSTARD) Serves 4, Vegetarian

INGREDIENTS

2 tablespoons sugar
2 (8-ounce) cans condensed milk
6 whole eggs
6 egg yolks
8 ounces heavy cream
2 ounces cognac

UTENSILS

1 flat-bottom stainless-steel bowl (1 gallon)
1 ceramic or glass bowl (1 gallon)
Metal whisk
Large roasting pan, at least 6 inches deep
Ceramic plate, large enough to cover
  stainless-steel bowl

PREPARATION

Preheat oven to 425°F. Put sugar into flat-bottom stainless-steel bowl. Place the bowl on the stove burner over medium heat. Stir gently with a wooden spoon over medium heat until sugar liquefies, then caramelizes. Perfect caramelized sugar should be a dark, amber color—almost the color of an old copper penny. Coat the sides of the bowl as high as possible with the caramelized sugar, then set aside to cool while you prep the egg mixture. (The caramelized sugar will end up on the top of the flan as a crispy sugar coating.)

In a glass or ceramic bowl, whisk condensed milk, eggs, egg yolks, heavy cream, and cognac, mixing well. Be sure to use all the condensed milk by scraping cans with a spatula.

Pour mixture into stainless-steel bowl that has caramelized sugar coating.

Bake at bain-marie* for 45–60 minutes, covering bowl with the ceramic plate to avoid water going into the mixture.

Remove from oven and cool at room temperature for at least an hour before moving to the refrigerator.

Transfer flan from stainless-steel bowl onto serving platter by placing the platter over the stainless steel bowl and flipping it gently.

*BAIN-MARIE PROCESS:

Place the stainless-steel bowl into a roasting pan or other baking vessel. For ample water circulation, the outside pan should be wide enough to leave a 1- to 2-inch edge around the inside bowl and the sides should be high enough to hold about an inch of water.

Pull the center rack halfway out of your preheated oven and carefully place the roasting pan on it.

Pour very hot tap water carefully into the roasting pan until the water reaches the level called for in the recipe—usually 1 inch high or halfway up the sides of the custard.

Gently slide the oven rack back into place, taking extra care not to slosh the water around.

When the custard is cooked, pull the rack halfway out again and carefully remove the bowl from the roasting pan.

CONVERSIONS

1 teaspoon	5 mL	1 ounce	28 g
1 tablespoon or 1/2 fluid ounce	15 mL	4 ounces or 1/4 pound	113 g
1 fluid ounce or 1/8 cup	30 mL	1/3 pound	150 g
1/4 cup or 2 fluid ounces	60 mL	8 ounces or 1/2 pound	230 g
1/3 cup	80 mL	2/3 pound	300 g
1/2 cup or 4 fluid ounces	120 mL	12 ounces or 3/4 pound	340 g
2/3 cup	160 mL	1 pound or 16 ounces	450 g
3/4 cup or 6 fluid ounces	180 mL	2 pounds	900 g
1 cup or 8 fluid ounces or half a pint	240 mL		
1 1/2 cups or 12 fluid ounces	350 mL		
2 cups or 1 pint or 16 fluid ounces	475 mL		
3 cups or 1 1/2 pints	715 mL		
4 cups or 2 pints or 1 quart	950 mL		
4 quarts or 1 gallon	3.8 L		

F Fahrenheit	C Celsius	F Fahrenheit	C Celsius
250	120	350	180
275	135	375	190
300	150	400	200
325	165	425	220

FRIENDS AND RESOURCES

Chef Ben Ford—www.chefbenford.com

Chef Bruce Sherman—www.northpondrestaurant.com

Chef Leonie McDonald—www.strictly-vegan.com

Just Label It—www.justlabelit.org

Hemp History Week—hemphistoryweek.com

CREDITS

Concept and words by Ziggy Marley

Food and style consultation by Karen Marley

Recipes by Ziggy Marley, Orly Marley, Karen Marley, Polin Agai, Chef Ben Ford, Chef Bruce Sherman, Chef Leonie McDonald, Chef Ricardo A. Rodríguez, Matt Solodky, and Lea Kabani

Executive produced by Orly Marley

Produced by Matt Solodky

Food styling by Caroline Hwang

Photography by Ryan Robert Miller

Photographs on pages 97 and 102 (bottom) by Kari Lovequist

Design and layout by Jeri Heiden, SMOG Design, Inc.

Editing by Johnny Temple/Akashic Books with Karen Marley and Matt Solodky

Hair by Shelee Maeda

Makeup by Danilo Cifuentes

ACKNOWLEDGMENTS

Family is more than me and mine, family is about all of us, the expanded human family. This book would not be possible without the support and contributions from my wife Orly, my children, my sister Karen, Chef Ben Ford, Chef Bruce Sherman, Chef Leonie McDonald, Chef Ricardo A. Rodríguez, Polin Agai, Lea Kabani, Matt Solodky, the team at Ziggy Marley Organics, and Johnny Temple and everyone at Akashic Books. Thank you all.

INDEX

ABOUT THE AUTHOR

Throughout the course of his three-decade career, Ziggy Marley has built a music legacy both alongside his siblings with Ziggy Marley & The Melody Makers (ten albums) and as a solo artist (six albums to date). As of 2016, Marley's music has garnered seven Grammy Awards and an Emmy; the humanitarian, singer, songwriter, and producer continually progresses at every turn. In 2012, he launched Ziggy Marley Organics, which includes a line of GMO-free coconut oils and hempseed snacks. Deeply committed to charity work, Ziggy leads U.R.G.E. (Unlimited Resources Giving Enlightenment), his nonprofit organization that focuses on uplifting children's lives through education around the world. He is also the author of the children's book *I Love You Too*, published by Akashic Books/Tuff Gong Worldwide.

Visit Ziggy online at **www.ziggymarley.com**. Follow Ziggy at: facebook.com/ziggymarley, instagram.com/ziggymarley, youtube.com/ziggymarley, and twitter.com/ziggymarley.